Content

CHAPTER 1: THE IMPORTANCE OF VISION IN LEADERSHIP 3
CHAPTER 2: DEVELOPING EMOTIONAL INTELLIGENCE 5
CHAPTER 3: EFFECTIVE COMMUNICATION AS A LEADER 7
CHAPTER 4: VALUES-BASED DECISION MAKING 9
CHAPTER 5: CHANGE MANAGEMENT AND ADAPTABILITY 11
CHAPTER 6: BUILDING HIGH PERFORMANCE TEAMS 13
CHAPTER 7: THE ART OF NEGOTIATION AND INFLUENCE 16
CHAPTER 8: ETHICAL LEADERSHIP AND SOCIAL RESPONSIBILITY 18
CHAPTER 9: DEVELOPING PERSONAL RESILIENCE 20
CHAPTER 10: TIME MANAGEMENT AND PRODUCTIVITY 22
CHAPTER 11: INNOVATION AND CREATIVE THINKING 24
CHAPTER 12: SERVANT LEADERSHIP: PUTTING OTHERS FIRST 26
CHAPTER 13: CONFLICT MANAGEMENT AND PROBLEM SOLVING 28
CHAPTER 14: PROMOTING DIVERSITY AND INCLUSION 30
CHAPTER 15: THE POWER OF EFFECTIVE DELEGATION 32
CHAPTER 16: DEVELOPING A POSITIVE FEEDBACK CULTURE 34
CHAPTER 17: THE IMPORTANCE OF AUTHENTICITY IN LEADERSHIP 36
CHAPTER 18: BUILDING AND MAINTAINING TRUST 38
CHAPTER 19: THE IMPORTANCE OF SELF-AWARENESS 40
CHAPTER 20: DEVELOPING A GROWTH MINDSET 42
CHAPTER 21: MANAGING EXPECTATIONS AND GOAL SETTING 44
CHAPTER 22: THE IMPORTANCE OF CURIOSITY AND CONTINUOUS LEARNING 46
CHAPTER 23: DEVELOPING COACHING SKILLS FOR LEADERS 48
CHAPTER 24: THE IMPORTANCE OF GRATITUDE IN LEADERSHIP 48
CHAPTER 25: LEADERSHIP AND STRESS MANAGEMENT 51
CHAPTER 26: THE IMPORTANCE OF PERSONAL DISCIPLINE 53
CHAPTER 27: DEVELOPING INTUITION FOR DECISION MAKING 55
CHAPTER 28: LEADERSHIP IN TIMES OF CRISIS 57
CHAPTER 29: THE IMPORTANCE OF HUMILITY IN LEADERSHIP 59

CHAPTER 30: DEVELOPING THE CAPACITY TO INFLUENCE WITHOUT AUTHORITY 61

CHAPTER 31: THE IMPORTANCE OF CLARITY AND SIMPLICITY 63

CHAPTER 32: DEVELOPING STRATEGIC PATIENCE 65

CHAPTER 33: LEADERSHIP AND THE IMPORTANCE OF PASSION 67

CHAPTER 34: THE IMPORTANCE OF CONSISTENCY IN LEADERSHIP 69

CHAPTER 35: DEVELOPING THE SKILL OF ACTIVE LISTENING 71

CHAPTER 36: THE IMPORTANCE OF FLEXIBILITY AND OPENNESS TO CHANGE 73

CHAPTER 37: DEVELOPING THE SKILL TO RECOGNIZE AND CELEBRATE ACCOMPLISHMENTS 75

Chapter 1: The Importance of Vision in Leadership

From ancient civilizations to modern corporations, history has shown that leaders with a clear and compelling vision are the ones who make the difference. Vision is more than a goal; It is a representation of our deepest aspirations, a picture of what could be, painted with the brushes of our hopes and dreams.

The Power of Vision

A powerful vision acts like a north star, providing direction and purpose. It is the promise of a better future that inspires people to push themselves beyond their perceived limits. When Martin Luther King Jr. gave his famous "I Have a Dream" speech, he was not simply sharing a goal, but a vision that resonated with millions and catalyzed a movement.

Developing a Vision

Developing a vision begins with introspection. What do you really value? What impact do you want to have in the world? The vision must be ambitious but achievable; challenging but realistic. It must be clear enough to be understood and shared by everyone, but flexible enough to adapt to changes.

Communicating the Vision

Once the vision is established, communicating it effectively is crucial. It should be a constant narrative in all the leader's communications. Every meeting, every email, every decision should reflect and reinforce the vision. Leaders like Steve Jobs were masters at this, using every opportunity to infuse their vision into Apple's culture.

Vision and Motivation

Vision is a powerful tool to motivate. It provides a sense of purpose that goes beyond daily tasks. When employees understand how their work contributes to a larger vision, they feel more engaged and satisfied. This is especially important in times of difficulty; The vision is the anchor that keeps the organization focused and on course.

Examples of Transformative Visions

Consider John F. Kennedy challenging the nation to put a man on the moon, or Elon Musk with his vision of colonizing Mars. These visions not only established clear goals, but also drove innovation and technological progress.

The Vision and the Leader

A leader with vision is someone who looks beyond the horizon. He is someone who sees opportunities where others see obstacles, and possibilities where others see problems. The leader's vision must be contagious, inspiring others to see and believe in a future that does not yet exist.

Conclusion

Vision is the art of seeing the invisible. It is the seed from which all great achievements grow. Without vision, leaders are mere administrators, trapped in the routine of everyday life. With vision, they become architects of the future, capable of building realities that previously only existed in the imagination.

Vision is, therefore, not only a part of leadership, but its very essence. It is what distinguishes a leader from a follower and what defines the legacy a leader leaves behind. Ultimately, vision is what makes the impossible possible.

Chapter 2: Developing Emotional Intelligence

Introduction to Emotional Intelligence

Emotional intelligence, a term popularized by psychologist Daniel Goleman, refers to the ability to identify and manage both our emotions and those of others. This skill is critical for leaders, as emotions play a crucial role in how we interact with others, make decisions, and deal with stress.

Self-awareness

The first step to developing emotional intelligence is self-awareness. It is the deep knowledge of our emotions, strengths, weaknesses, values and motivations. A self-aware leader is able to reflect on her actions and decisions, and understand how these affect her team and environment.

Self-management

Once we are aware of our emotions, the next step is to learn to manage them. Self-management involves controlling impulses, managing stress in a healthy way, and maintaining a positive attitude even in adverse situations. A leader who masters self-management can remain calm and clear under pressure.

Empathy

Empathy is the ability to understand and share the feelings of another. In leadership, empathy allows us to create deep connections with the team, understand their challenges and motivations, and respond appropriately to their needs. An empathetic leader is seen as understanding and approachable, which fosters a positive and collaborative work environment.

Social skills

Social skills are the final component of emotional intelligence. They include the ability to communicate clearly, resolve conflicts, inspire and persuade others, and build lasting relationships. A leader with strong social skills can mobilize her team toward common goals and maintain a strong support network.

Continuous development

Developing emotional intelligence is a continuous process. It requires practice, feedback, and a willingness to step out of your comfort zone. Leaders can improve their emotional intelligence through meditation, reflection, coaching, and training in communication and conflict resolution skills.

Conclusion

Emotional intelligence is more than a soft skill; It is a powerful tool that can transform the way we lead, work and live. By developing our emotional intelligence, we not only improve our relationships and well-being, but we also increase our ability to lead with compassion, clarity, and courage.

Chapter 3: Effective Communication as a Leader

The Essence of Communication in Leadership

Effective communication in leadership transcends the simple exchange of information. It is the art of conveying visions, values and goals in a way that resonates with others. An effective leader knows that communication is two-way; not only speaks, but actively listens, showing empathy and understanding towards the perspectives of others.

Principles of Effective Communication

To communicate effectively, leaders must adhere to certain principles:

Clarity: Being clear and concise avoids misunderstandings and keeps everyone on the same page.

Consistency: Maintaining a consistent message reinforces the vision and values of the organization.

Authenticity: Being genuine and transparent fosters trust and credibility.

Empathy: Understanding and recognizing others' emotions improves connection and collaboration.

Feedback: Offering and receiving constructive feedback is essential for growth and continuous improvement.

Tools to Improve Communication

Leaders can use various tools to improve their communication:

Active listening: Pay full attention to the interlocutor, showing interest and responding appropriately.

Body language: Use gestures and facial expressions to reinforce the verbal message.

Storytelling: Tell stories that illustrate key points and make the message memorable.

Open questions: Encourage participation and dialogue through questions that invite reflection and discussion.

Technology: Use digital tools to improve remote communication and ensure that everyone has access to information.

Common Challenges in Communication

Even the most experienced leaders can face communication challenges:

Cultural Barriers: Navigating cultural and linguistic differences to ensure the message is universally understood.

Resistance to change: Overcome teams' reluctance to accept new ideas or directions.

Information Overload: Avoid communication fatigue by ensuring messages are timely and relevant.

Conclusion

Effective communication is vital to leadership. It's not just about talking and listening, but about understanding and connecting. Leaders who master the art of communication can inspire trust, motivate their teams, and successfully lead toward achieving common goals.

Chapter 4: Values-Based Decision Making

Introduction

In a world full of options and divergent paths, the ability to make wise and ethical decisions is more crucial than ever. For leaders, the decisions they make can have a significant impact on people's lives and the destiny of their organizations. Therefore, it is essential that these decisions are based on a solid set of values.

Defining Values

Values are the fundamental principles that guide our behavior. They are the internal compass that guides us in the right direction when we face moral crossroads. In the context of leadership, values may include integrity, honesty, responsibility, respect, fairness, and compassion.

The Values-Based Decision Making Process

Values-based decision making involves several key steps:

Identification of Securities: Recognize and clearly define personal and organizational values.

Options Evaluation: Consider how each option aligns with these values.

Consequence Analysis: Reflect on the long-term implications of each decision for all stakeholders.

Stock Selection: Choose the course of action that best reflects the identified values.

Review and Reflection: Evaluate the decisions made and learn from them for future situations.

Values in Action

Leaders who practice values-based decision making often find their teams are more engaged and motivated. Employees tend to follow leaders who act in accordance with their values, as this creates a work environment in which they feel valued and respected.

Challenges and Solutions

Values-based decision making is not without its challenges. Sometimes values can conflict, or external pressures can make it difficult to stay true to them. In these cases, it is important for leaders to have a clear process and to seek advice from trusted mentors or advisors.

Conclusion

Values-based decision making is a powerful practice that can transform leadership and organizational culture. By adhering to a clear set of values, leaders can navigate the complex world of decision-making with confidence and clarity, ensuring that their actions benefit not only their organizations, but also society at large.

Chapter 5: Change Management and Adaptability

The Nature of Change

Change is a constant in life and business. It can be disruptive and disconcerting, but it is also an opportunity for growth and innovation. Leaders must recognize that change management is not a one-time event, but rather an ongoing process that requires vision, patience, and persistence.

Principles of Change Management

To manage change effectively, leaders must adhere to certain principles:

Clear Communication: Inform all stakeholders about the nature of the change, the 'why' behind it and how it will be implemented.

Active participation: Involve team members in the change process to foster acceptance and commitment.

Support and Training: Provide the tools and training necessary for employees to adapt to new ways of working.

Expectation Management: Set realistic expectations and prepare for challenges that may arise.

Celebration of Successes: Recognize and celebrate achievements to maintain high morale and reinforce the culture of change.

Developing Adaptability

Adaptability is the ability to adjust quickly to new conditions. Adaptive leaders are proactive, resilient, and open to new ideas. They encourage experimentation and learning from mistakes, and see failure as an opportunity to improve.

Continuous Learning Culture

A culture of continuous learning is essential for adaptability. Leaders must foster an environment where curiosity and the pursuit of knowledge are valued and where employees feel safe to explore and try new ideas.

Conclusion

Change management and adaptability are not just desirable skills, but critical needs in contemporary leadership. Leaders who master these skills can navigate change with confidence, inspire their teams to embrace new opportunities, and ensure their organizations not only survive, but thrive in an ever-evolving environment.

Chapter 6: Building High Performance Teams

Introduction

High-performing teams are the engine of successful organizations. These teams are characterized by their ability to work together toward a common goal, overcoming obstacles and achieving exceptional results. Building these teams is one of the most important responsibilities of a leader.

Fundamentals of High Performance Teams

To develop a high-performing team, leaders must establish a solid foundation that includes:

Clear objectives: Define clear, achievable goals that provide direction and purpose.

Defined Roles: Ensure that each team member knows their role and how they contribute to the team's success.

Mutual trust: Foster an environment where trust is the basis of team relationships.

Open Communication: Promote transparency and the exchange of ideas without fear of reprisals.

Collective Responsibility: Establish a culture where achievements and failures are shared by everyone.

Leadership in High Performance Teams

Leadership is key in building and maintaining high-performing teams. Effective leaders:

Inspire Vision: They share a clear vision that motivates and guides the team.

Empower Members: They delegate authority and encourage independent decision making.

They promote innovation: They create a safe space for experimentation and learning.

They Recognize Performance: They celebrate successes and provide constructive feedback.

Develop Skills: They invest in the professional and personal development of team members.

High Performance Culture

A high-performance culture is one that values excellence, commitment and continuous improvement. To cultivate this culture, leaders must:

Model Behavior: Be an example of the values and standards expected of the team.

Foster Collaboration: Encourage teamwork and mutual help.

Manage Conflict: Address challenges in a constructive and timely manner.

Maintain Agility: Adapt quickly to changes and keep the team focused on priorities.

Challenges and Strategies

Building high-performing teams is not without challenges. Leaders may face resistance to change, interpersonal conflicts, and external pressures. To overcome these challenges, it is crucial to:

Communicate Effectively: Maintain clear and consistent lines of communication.

Build Resilience: Help the team develop the ability to recover from setbacks.

Promote Diversity: Value and take advantage of different perspectives and skills.

Evaluate and Adjust: Conduct periodic reviews and adjust strategies as necessary.

Conclusion

High-performing teams are the result of intentional leadership and management practices focused on excellence. By following the principles and strategies outlined in this chapter, leaders can build teams that not only meet their goals but also set new standards for success.

Chapter 7: The Art of Negotiation and Influence

Negotiation and influencing are essential skills in all areas of life. This chapter dives into how we can improve these skills to achieve our goals and foster positive relationships.

Understanding Negotiation

Negotiation is a two-way communication process designed to reach an agreement when you and another party have some shared and other opposing interests.

Principles of Effective Negotiation

Preparation: Know your objectives, alternatives, and the best alternative to a negotiated agreement (BATNA).

Active listening: Really understand what the other party needs and wants.

Clear communication: Express your needs and desires directly and respectfully.

Flexibility: Be willing to adapt and change your approach if necessary.

Win-win solutions: Find agreements that benefit both parties.

The Psychology of Influence

Understanding how people make decisions is key to influencing them. This includes knowledge of psychological principles such as reciprocity, consistency, social proof, authority, scarcity, and agreeableness.

Influence Tactics

Reciprocity: The tendency to return favors.

Commitment and consistency: The need to be consistent with what we have said or done previously.

Social proof: The influence of seeing others do the same.

Authority: The tendency to follow the leadership of authority figures.

Shortage: We value more what is less available.

Sympathy: We are more influenced by people we like.

Negotiation in Practice

Study cases: Analysis of successful and failed historical negotiations.

Role-playing: Negotiation simulations to practice skills.

Advanced strategies: Techniques such as anchoring and framing.

Building Lasting Relationships

The negotiation does not end when an agreement is reached. Maintaining and building relationships is essential for future successful negotiations.

Conclusion

Mastering the art of negotiation and influence can open doors and create opportunities. Through understanding, practicing and applying these skills, we can achieve extraordinary results.

Chapter 8: Ethical Leadership and Social Responsibility

Ethical leadership and social responsibility are fundamental pillars for building sustainable organizations and just societies. This chapter focuses on how leaders can cultivate these essential qualities.

The Essence of Ethical Leadership

Ethical leadership is based on integrity, honesty and commitment to justice. It is the art of influencing and guiding others with principles that promote the common good.

Principles of Ethical Leadership

Integrity: Be consistent in words and actions.

Transparency: Communicate openly and honestly.

Equity: Treat everyone fairly and without prejudice.

Responsibility: Assume responsibility for decisions and their consequences.

Corporate Social Responsibility (CSR)

CSR refers to business practices that take into account the social, economic and environmental impact of the company. It involves going beyond legal compliance and actively contributing to the well-being of society and the environment.

Strategies to Implement CSR

Green initiatives: Reduce the carbon footprint and promote sustainability.

Labor inclusion: Promote diversity and equal opportunities in the workplace.

Philanthropy: Support social and community causes through donations and volunteering.

The Impact of Ethical Leadership and CSR

Ethically led organizations with strong CSR tend to enjoy a better reputation, greater employee and customer loyalty, and often better long-term financial performance.

Challenges and Solutions

Conflicts of interest: Establish clear policies and control mechanisms.

Performance pressures: Balance short-term goals with long-term vision.

Cultural change: Create an organizational culture that values ethics and social responsibility.

The Role of Leaders in CSR

Leaders must be champions of CSR, setting an example to follow and motivating others to adopt responsible practices.

Conclusion

Ethical leadership and social responsibility are not just business strategies, but personal commitments that reflect our deepest values. By embracing these principles, leaders can inspire change and have a lasting positive impact on the world.

Chapter 9: Developing Personal Resilience

Resilience is the ability to quickly recover from difficulties; It is a vital skill in a world that is constantly changing and full of uncertainties. This chapter focuses on how we can strengthen our personal resilience.

Understanding Resilience

Resilience is not an innate quality, but rather a skill that can be developed and strengthened with practice and determination. It is the combination of mental, emotional and physical resistance.

Factors that Contribute to Resilience

- **Optimism**: Maintain a positive perspective in the face of challenges.
- **Flexibility**: Adapt to new situations and learn from them.
- **Support net**: Have a strong support system of family and friends.

Strategies to Develop Resilience

- **Self-knowledge**: Understand your own reactions and emotions.
- **Self-care**: Prioritize your physical and mental well-being.
- **Positive coping**: Face problems constructively and proactively.

Resilience in Action

- **Examples of life**: Stories of people who have overcome significant adversity.
- **Practical exercises**: Activities designed to strengthen resilience.
- **Tools and resources**: Mindfulness techniques, gratitude journals and more.

Overcoming obstacles

Resilience helps us navigate life's obstacles, learning and growing from each experience.

The Role of the Leader in Resilience

Resilient leaders are able to guide others through difficult times and foster an environment of strength and adaptability.

Conclusion

Developing personal resilience is an ongoing journey that prepares us to face life's challenges with grace and strength. By adopting these practices, we can live a fuller and more satisfying life.

Chapter 10: Time Management and Productivity

Effective time management and improving productivity are crucial skills in a fast-paced world. This chapter focuses on how we can optimize our time to achieve more with less stress.

Understanding Time Management

Time management is not about doing more things in less time, but about doing the right things efficiently and effectively.

Principles of Effective Time Management

- **Priorization**: Identify what really matters and dedicate time and resources to it.
- **Planning**: Set clear goals and design a plan to achieve them.
- **Delegation**: Know when and to whom to delegate tasks to be more efficient.

Tools and Techniques to Improve Productivity

- **Pomodoro Method**: Work in blocks of time with regular breaks.
- **80/20 Rule**: Focus on the 20% of the tasks that produce 80% of the results.
- **Five Seconds Technique by Mel Robbins**: Overcome procrastination by taking immediate action.

The Psychology of Productivity

Understanding how our motivation and habits work can help us be more productive.

Overcoming Procrastination

- **Identify the causes**: Understanding why we procrastinate is the first step to overcoming it.

- **Coping strategies**: Develop techniques to manage the tendency to postpone.

The Role of the Environment in Productivity

- **Work space**: Create an environment that encourages concentration and efficiency.
- **Organizational culture**: Promote practices that support collective productivity.

Balance between Life and Work

Managing time effectively also means finding a healthy balance between work and personal life.

Conclusion

Time management and productivity are not just about working harder, they are about working smarter. By adopting these strategies, we can live a more balanced and fulfilling life.

Chapter 11: Innovation and Creative Thinking

Innovation and creative thinking are engines of change and progress. This chapter explores how we can unlock our creative potential and foster an innovative mindset.

Defining Innovation and Creativity

- **Innovation**: The implementation of new or significantly improved ideas.
- **Creativity**: The ability to generate original and valuable ideas.

Key Elements of Creative Thinking

- **Curiosity**: Actively seek new experiences and knowledge.
- **Opening**: Be willing to consider different ideas and perspectives.
- **Flexibility**: Adapt and think about alternatives and possibilities.

Fostering a Creative Environment

- **inspiring spaces**: Design environments that stimulate creativity.
- **Innovation culture**: Create a culture that values and rewards innovation.

Techniques to Stimulate Creativity

- **Brainstorming**: Generate many ideas without judging them initially.
- **Lateral thinking**: Approach problems from unusual angles.
- **Mental maps**: Visualize ideas and their interconnection.

Innovation in Practice

- **Prototype development**: Create initial versions of products or services to test and improve.
- **Iteration**: Continuously improve through feedback and refinement cycles.
- **Technology adoption**: Use emerging tools and technologies to drive innovation.

Overcoming Creative Blocks

- **Unlocking exercises**: Activities designed to overcome mental barriers.
- **Rest and fun**: Recognize the importance of leisure and play in creativity.

The Role of the Leader in Innovation

- **Model to follow**: Be an example of creative and innovative thinking.
- **Facilitator**: Provide resources and support for experimentation.

Conclusion

Innovation and creative thinking are essential skills in the 21st century. By fostering these skills, we can solve complex problems and create a brighter, more sustainable future.

Chapter 12: Servant Leadership: Putting Others First

Servant leadership focuses on the well-being and growth of others. This chapter explores how leaders can adopt this philosophy to create more collaborative and empathetic work environments.

Definition of Servant Leadership

- **Servant leadership**: A leadership approach that prioritizes the needs of others before one's own, seeking to serve rather than be served.

Principles of Servant Leadership

- **Actively listen**: Pay full attention to the concerns and needs of others.
- **Empathy**: Understand and share the feelings of others.
- **Growth of others**: Promote the personal and professional development of team members.

Benefits of Servant Leadership

- **Trust culture**: Build relationships based on trust and mutual respect.
- **Greater commitment**: Teams with servant leaders tend to show greater commitment and job satisfaction.
- **Continuous improvement**: A focus on service leads to a constant search for improvements and learning.

Implementation of Servant Leadership

- **Model to follow**: Be an example of service and dedication.
- **Mentoring**: Offer guidance and support for the growth of others.
- **Effective delegation**: Empower others to make decisions and assume responsibilities.

Challenges and Solutions

- **Balance between service and direction**: Find the right balance between serving and leading.
- **Expectation management**: Ensure that the intention to serve is not confused with the inability to make difficult decisions.

The Role of the Servant Leader in Times of Crisis

- **Support and guidance**: Provide stability and direction during uncertain times.
- **Resilience**: Demonstrate strength and optimism to inspire others.

Conclusion

Servant leadership is a powerful form of influence that puts people first. By taking this approach, leaders can transform their organizations and foster a sense of community and purpose.

Chapter 13: Conflict Management and Problem Solving

On the path to personal and professional success, we inevitably encounter conflicts and problems that require our attention and resolution. How we handle these challenges can define our path and significantly affect our relationships and well-being.

The Nature of Conflict

Conflict is a natural part of the human experience. It arises from differences in values, motivations, perceptions, desires or experiences. Accepting that conflict is a normal part of life is the first step to managing it effectively.

Understanding Perspectives

To resolve a conflict, it is essential to understand the perspectives of all parties involved. This doesn't just mean listening, but also striving to truly understand the other's point of view, even if we don't agree with it.

Effective communication

Communication is the most powerful tool in conflict resolution. Clear, open and honest communication can prevent misunderstandings that often lead to conflict. It is important to express our thoughts and feelings in a way that they are received without provoking defensiveness.

Resolution Strategies

There are multiple strategies to resolve conflicts, including negotiation, mediation and, in some cases, arbitration. The key is to find common ground and work towards a solution that is acceptable to all parties.

The Importance of Ethics and Empathy

Acting with integrity and empathy is crucial in conflict management. Understanding and respecting the feelings and positions of others, while staying true to one's own ethical principles, can lead to more lasting and satisfying resolutions.

The Role of Leadership

Leaders play a vital role in conflict resolution. They must be able to identify conflicts, understand underlying causes, and facilitate a resolution process that promotes harmony and collaboration.

Building Resilience

Conflict resolution also involves building resilience. Learning from past conflicts and using those lessons to better handle future challenges is an important part of personal and professional growth.

Conclusion

Conflict management and problem solving are not only necessary skills, but opportunities to strengthen relationships and foster a collaborative and respectful work environment. By approaching conflict with an open and constructive mindset, we can transform challenges into opportunities for development and continuous improvement.

Chapter 14: Promoting Diversity and Inclusion

Diversity and inclusion are more than just business policies; They are foundations that can transform organizations and societies. This chapter explores how we can create environments where each person feels valued and an integral part of the whole.

Understanding Diversity

Diversity encompasses individual differences in race, gender, age, sexual orientation, disability, religion, life experience, and more. Recognizing and valuing these differences is the first step towards inclusion.

Inclusion as a Practice

Inclusion is the practice of ensuring that all people have access to the same opportunities and are able to contribute fully to their communities. It is an active commitment to recognize and embrace diversity.

Barriers to Diversity and Inclusion

Despite progress, there are still barriers that prevent full diversity and inclusion. These can be structural, such as organizational policies and practices, or interpersonal, such as prejudices and stereotypes.

Strategies to Promote Diversity and Inclusion

To overcome these barriers, strategies such as mentoring programs, unconscious bias training, and inclusive recruitment policies can be implemented. The key is the conscious and deliberate implementation of these strategies.

The Impact of Diversity and Inclusion

Organizations that embrace diversity and inclusion are not only more fair and equitable, but also benefit from greater creativity, innovation and performance.

The Role of Leaders

Leaders have a responsibility to be role models in promoting diversity and inclusion. They must lead by example, educate others, and advocate for meaningful change.

Building Inclusive Cultures

Creating an inclusive culture requires constant effort and participation from all members of the organization. It is a continuous process that is nourished by education, reflection and action.

Conclusion

Fostering diversity and inclusion is a never-ending journey, but one that has the power to transform. By committing to these principles, we can build a world where every person has the opportunity to reach their full potential.

Chapter 15: The Power of Effective Delegation

Effective delegation is a key tool for leaders and managers, allowing you to optimize resources and enhance the team's skills. This chapter addresses how to delegate in ways that empower employees and improve productivity.

Understanding Delegation

Delegation is not simply assigning tasks; It is an act of trust and recognition of the capabilities of others.

Principles of Effective Delegation

- **Clarity**: Define objectives and expectations precisely.
- **Adequacy**: Assign tasks according to each person's skills and experience.
- **Authority**: Grant the necessary authority to make decisions relevant to the task.

Delegation Benefits

- **Skill development**: Promote the professional growth of the team.
- **Efficiency**: Improve workload distribution and overall productivity.
- **Leadership**: Strengthen leadership capacity by focusing on strategic tasks.

Barriers to Delegation

- **Micromanagement**: The tendency to over-supervise can undermine delegation.
- **Fear to fail**: Worry about mistakes can prevent effective delegation.

Overcoming Obstacles in the Delegation

- **Trust**: Build relationships based on mutual trust.
- **Communication**: Maintain open lines of communication for support and feedback.

The Delegation Process

- **Task identification**: Determine which tasks are delegable.
- **Delegate selection**: Choose the right people for the tasks.
- **Monitoring and feedback**: Evaluate progress and provide constructive feedback.

The Role of the Leader in the Delegation

- **Model to follow**: Demonstrate good delegation practices.
- **Mentoring**: Offer guidance and support to facilitate delegation.

Conclusion

Effective delegation is a manifestation of intelligent and thoughtful leadership. By delegating properly, leaders can improve efficiency, develop their team, and achieve better results.

Chapter 16: Developing a Positive Feedback Culture

Positive feedback is a powerful tool for development and continuous improvement. This chapter focuses on how we can establish and nurture a culture that values and uses constructive feedback.

The Importance of Positive Feedback

Positive feedback not only recognizes achievements, but also motivates and guides future development. It is essential for a healthy and productive work environment.

Principles of Positive Feedback

- **Specific**: Be clear and specific about what is being praised.
- **Prompt**: Give feedback shortly after the action to make it more relevant.
- **Balanced**: Combine praise with suggestions for improvement.

Creating an Open Feedback Environment

- **Model to follow**: Leaders must practice what they preach by giving and receiving feedback.
- **Clear rules**: Set expectations about how and when feedback is given.
- **Training**: Teach employees how to give and receive feedback effectively.

Benefits of a Feedback Culture

- **Continuous improvement**: Positive feedback encourages reflection and personal growth.
- **Strengthened relationships**: Constructive feedback can improve communication and trust.
- **Improved performance**: Teams that practice feedback regularly tend to be more efficient and effective.

Overcoming Barriers to Feedback

- **Fear of conflict**: Address the anxiety that may arise when giving or receiving feedback.
- **Receptivity**: Encourage an open mindset to accept feedback.

The Process of Giving Feedback

- **Preparation**: Reflect on the purpose and objectives of the feedback.
- **Communication**: Use positive and constructive language.
- **Follow-up**: Discuss steps and strategies for implementing suggestions.

The Leader's Role in Feedback

- **Facilitator**: Create opportunities for feedback to flow in all directions.
- **Mentor**: Offer guidance and support to interpret and act on feedback.

Conclusion

Developing a positive feedback culture is a dynamic process that requires commitment and practice. By fostering this culture, we can create environments where everyone feels valued and empowered to reach their full potential.

Chapter 17: The Importance of Authenticity in Leadership

Authenticity in leadership is essential to building genuine relationships and fostering a transparent and honest work environment. This chapter focuses on how leaders can be authentic and why it is crucial to their effectiveness.

Defining Authenticity

Authenticity is being true to yourself, aligning actions and words with personal values and beliefs. It is honesty applied to interaction with others.

Benefits of Authenticity

- **Trust**: Authentic leaders inspire trust and loyalty in their teams.
- **Strong relationships**: Authenticity fosters deeper, more meaningful relationships.
- **Better decision making**: Clarity in values and principles leads to more consistent and ethical decisions.

Developing Authenticity

- **Self-knowledge**: Understand your own values, strengths and weaknesses.
- **Vulnerability**: Show your humanity and admit mistakes when necessary.
- **Consistency**: Stick to your principles even when it's difficult.

Authenticity and Diversity

- **Inclusion**: Value and respect individual differences within the team.
- **Model to follow**: Be an example of how diversity of thought and experience enriches leadership.

Challenges of Authenticity

- **Perceptions**: Manage how others view authenticity and its implications.
- **Balance**: Find the balance between being open and maintaining professionalism.

The Role of the Authentic Leader

- **Inspiration**: Motivate others to also be authentic and open.
- **Mentoring**: Guide others on their own journey toward authenticity.

Conclusion

Authenticity is an invaluable quality in leadership. By being authentic, leaders not only improve their own effectiveness, but also create a culture of openness and honesty that can transform the entire organization.

Chapter 18: Building and Maintaining Trust

Trust is the foundation of all successful relationships. This chapter focuses on how we can build trust effectively and maintain it over time.

The Nature of Trust

Trust is a belief in the reliability, truth, ability or strength of someone or something. It is an intangible element, but its presence or absence is deeply felt in all human interactions.

Key Elements to Building Trust

- **Integrity**: Be honest and consistent in your actions and words.
- **Competence**: Demonstrate skill and knowledge in your work area.
- **Consistency**: Act predictably and reliably over time.

Strategies to Develop Confidence

- **Open communication**: Encourage honest and transparent dialogue.
- **Controlled vulnerability**: Share your thoughts and feelings in a way that invites others to do the same.
- **Promises kept**: Make sure you meet your commitments and expectations.

Maintaining Trust

- **Mutual respect**: Value and consider the opinions and needs of others.
- **Responsibility**: Accept your mistakes and work to correct them.
- **Support**: Be present for others, especially in difficult times.

Rebuilding Broken Trust

- **Recognition of damage**: Accept and understand the impact of actions that broke trust.
- **Repair process**: Take concrete steps to repair the damage and restore trust.
- **Patience**: Understand that rebuilding trust takes time and effort.

The Leader's Role in Trust

- **Model to follow**: Be an example of reliability and transparency.
- **Trust culture**: Create an environment where trust is a value shared and practiced by all.

Conclusion

Building and maintaining trust is an ongoing process that requires dedication and commitment. By focusing on integrity, competence and consistency, we can build strong, lasting relationships that will stand the tests of time.

Chapter 19: The Importance of Self-Awareness

Self-awareness is the deep knowledge of our thoughts, emotions, motivations and behaviors. It is a critical skill that allows individuals to understand themselves and how they interact with others.

Understanding Self-Awareness

- **Definition**: Recognize your own internal states, preferences, resources and intuitions.
- **Self appraisal**: Learn to observe and reflect on your own emotions and reactions.

Benefits of Self-Awareness

- **Better decision making**: Understanding your motivations helps you make decisions that are more aligned with your values.
- **Stronger relationships**: Self-awareness improves empathy and understanding in relationships.
- **Personal development**: Facilitates personal growth and emotional self-regulation.

Developing Self-Awareness

- **Mindfulness**: Practice mindfulness to be present and aware of your thoughts and feelings.
- **Personal diary**: Write regularly about your experiences and emotions to discover patterns and triggers.
- **Feedback**: Seek constructive feedback from others to gain outside perspectives.

Self-awareness in Leaders and Coaches

- **Model to follow**: Self-aware leaders are better able to guide others and foster an environment of openness.

- **Effective coaching**: Self-awareness allows coaches to understand and connect with their clients on a deeper level.

Challenges and Solutions

- **Defensiveness**: Learn to accept criticism without reacting defensively.
- **Self-deception**: Recognize and overcome internal narratives that distort reality.

The Role of Self-Awareness in Change

- **Behavioral change**: Use self-awareness to identify and modify unwanted behaviors.
- **Continuous growth**: View self-awareness as a lifelong practice for personal development.

Conclusion

Self-awareness is a cornerstone of human development. By fostering this skill, we can live more intentionally, build more meaningful relationships, and lead with greater empathy and clarity.

Chapter 20: Developing a Growth Mindset

Growth mindset is the belief that our abilities and understanding can be developed with effort and dedication. This chapter focuses on how we can cultivate this mindset to achieve our goals and overcome obstacles.

Understanding the Growth Mindset

- **Definition**: Contrasts with the fixed mindset, which assumes that our abilities are static.
- **Importance**: The growth mindset allows us to see challenges as opportunities to learn and grow.

Principles of Growth Mindset

- **Strive to learn**: Value the learning process over the result.
- **Persistence**: Maintain effort despite obstacles and failures.
- **Flexibility**: Be willing to change strategy when something doesn't work.

Fostering a Growth Mindset

- **Praise the effort**: Recognize hard work and dedication more than results.
- **Model learning**: Share your own experiences of learning and growth.
- **Set challenging goals**: Encourage setting goals that require effort and learning.

Growth Mindset in Practice

- **Exercises and activities**: Provide tasks that promote critical thinking and problem solving.
- **Reflection and self-assessment**: Encourage reflection on the learning process itself.

Overcoming Fixed Mindset

- **Identify limiting beliefs**: Recognize and challenge the ideas that prevent us from growing.
- **Internal dialogue change**: Transform negative self-talk into one that supports growth.

The Role of the Leader in Promoting the Growth Mindset

- **Inspiration**: Motivate others to adopt a growth mindset.
- **Support**: Provide resources and opportunities for personal and professional development.

Conclusion

Developing a growth mindset is a transformative journey that opens up a world of possibilities. By embracing this mindset, we can overcome perceived limitations and achieve levels of success and satisfaction we never imagined possible.

Chapter 21: Managing Expectations and Goal Setting

Managing expectations and setting goals are essential skills for achieving goals and maintaining motivation. This chapter focuses on how we can set realistic goals and manage our expectations to maximize success.

Understanding Expectation Management

- **Definition**: The ability to anticipate and control the perception of future results.
- **Realism**: Adjust our expectations to what is feasible and achievable.

Benefits of Effective Expectation Management

- **Satisfaction**: Avoid disappointment by aligning expectations with reality.
- **Motivation**: Maintain motivation by having clear and realistic expectations.

Developing Goal Setting

- **SMART goals**: Establish Specific, Measurable, Attainable, Relevant and Temporal goals.
- **Planning**: Design a detailed action plan to achieve each goal.

Strategies to Manage Expectations

- **Communication**: Be clear and transparent about what to expect.
- **Flexibility**: Be prepared to adjust expectations as circumstances change.

Goal Setting in Practice

- **Display**: Use visualization to see the success of goals.

- **Follow-up**: Monitor progress and adjust goals as necessary.

Overcoming Disappointment

- **Acceptance**: Recognize that not all expectations will always be met.
- **Learning**: See each experience as an opportunity to learn and grow.

Conclusion

Managing expectations and setting goals are dynamic processes that require continuous attention and adjustment. By mastering these skills, we can improve our ability to achieve success and stay motivated along the way.

Chapter 22: The Importance of Curiosity and Continuous Learning

Introduction

In a rapidly changing world, curiosity and continuous learning emerge as crucial skills for personal and professional growth. This chapter explores how to foster curiosity and create a habit of lifelong learning.

Curiosity as a Driver of Learning: Curiosity is the spark that ignites the search for knowledge. It is an innate quality that drives us to explore the unknown and question what is established. As life coaching experts, we must encourage our coachees to embrace their natural curiosity and view every question as a learning opportunity.

Developing the Continuous Learning Mindset: Continuous learning is the process of constantly acquiring new skills or knowledge. To develop this mindset, it is essential to adopt an attitude of humility and recognize that there is always something new to learn, no matter how expert you are in a field.

Strategies to Keep Curiosity Alive:

1. **Powerful Questions:** Ask questions that challenge assumptions and open new perspectives.

2. **Active Exploration:** Engage in activities that expand your horizons, such as traveling, reading, or attending workshops.

3. **Deep Reflection:** Take time to reflect on experiences and lessons learned.

Benefits of Continuous Learning: Continuous learning not only enriches our knowledge, but also improves our adaptability, increases our network of professional contacts and opens doors to new opportunities.

Conclusion: Curiosity and continuous learning are essential to staying relevant and competitive in any field. As motivational speakers, our role is to inspire others to never stop learning and to keep the flame of curiosity alive.

Chapter 23: Developing Coaching Skills for Leaders

Introduction

Effective leadership is essential in any organization. This chapter focuses on how leaders can develop coaching skills to improve their leadership and foster an environment of continuous growth and development in their teams.

The Role of the Leader as a Coach: A leader with coaching skills not only directs, but also inspires, motivates and empowers his team. The leader-coach adopts a person-centered approach, facilitating the personal and professional development of team members.

Key Coaching Skills for Leaders:

1. **Active listening:** Pay full attention to the interlocutor, understanding not only the words, but also the underlying feelings and thoughts.

2. **Effective Questions:** Use open questions that promote reflection and exploration of ideas and solutions.

3. **Constructive Feedback:** Offer feedback that is specific, objective, and growth-oriented.

Developing a Coaching Mindset: To be an effective leader-coach, it is crucial to adopt a coaching mindset that values curiosity, openness to change, and continuous improvement. This means being willing to learn from others and seeing mistakes as learning opportunities.

Implementing Coaching in Daily Practice: Leaders can incorporate coaching into their daily routine through one-on-one meetings, brainstorming sessions, and setting personalized development goals for each team member.

Conclusion: Coaching skills are a powerful tool for any leader. By developing these skills, leaders can create stronger, more resilient and adaptive teams, capable of meeting the challenges of the future.

Chapter 24: The Importance of Gratitude in Leadership

Introduction

Gratitude is more than a courtesy; It is a powerful leadership tool that can transform teams and organizations. This chapter addresses how leaders can cultivate and express gratitude to improve team morale, collaboration, and performance.

The Power of Gratitude: Gratitude in leadership not only recognizes effort and achievement, but also fosters a positive and supportive environment. Leaders who practice gratitude inspire loyalty and motivation, leading to greater commitment and job satisfaction.

Cultivating a Culture of Gratitude:

1. **Public recognition:** Celebrate team members' successes and contributions in company meetings or communications.
2. **Personalized Appreciation:** Offer personalized thanks that reflect awareness of individual contributions.
3. **Daily Gratitude Practices:** Integrate moments of gratitude into your daily routine, such as thanking someone each day or keeping a gratitude journal.

Gratitude and Resilience: Gratitude also plays a crucial role in team resilience. Recognizing challenges overcome and lessons learned strengthens the team's ability to face future obstacles.

Implementing Gratitude Strategies: Leaders can implement gratitude strategies through training, coaching, and modeling behaviors. This includes everything from gratitude workshops to coaching sessions where skills related to gratitude are practiced.

Conclusion

Gratitude is an expression of recognition that goes beyond words; It is an action that builds and maintains solid relationships. As leaders and motivational speakers, we must be examples of gratitude, showing how this powerful tool can lead to stronger, more successful teams.

Chapter 25: Leadership and Stress Management

Introduction

Stress is an omnipresent phenomenon in the modern workplace. For leaders, managing their own stress and that of their teams is crucial to maintaining a healthy and productive work environment. This chapter explores the techniques and strategies that leaders can employ to manage stress effectively.

Understanding Stress:

- **Definition and Causes:** Exploration of what stress is and what factors cause it in the work context.
- **Positive Stress vs. Negative:** Differentiation between eustress that motivates and distress that paralyzes.

The Impact of Stress on Leadership:

- **Effects on Decision Making:** How stress can affect judgment and the ability to make clear decisions.
- **Stress and Communication:** The role of stress in effective communication within teams.

Self-Assessment Tools:

- **Identification of Symptoms:** Techniques to recognize signs of stress in oneself and others.
- **Evaluations and Surveys:** Use of tools to measure stress levels and their impact.

Stress Management Techniques for Leaders:

- **Mindfulness and Meditation:** Implementing mindfulness practices to reduce anxiety.
- **Time management:** Strategies for efficient time management that minimizes stress.

- **Effective Delegation:** Learn to delegate responsibilities to avoid work overload.

Promoting Resilience in Teams:

- **Resilience Training:** Development of programs to strengthen team resilience.
- **Supportive Culture:** Creating a work environment that promotes mutual support and collaboration.

Organizational Strategies:

- **Wellness Policies:** Implementation of policies that promote well-being and reduce work stress.
- **Employee Support Resources:** Availability of resources such as counseling and stress management workshops.

Conclusion: Effective leadership requires the ability to manage your own stress and that of others. By taking a proactive approach and equipping leaders with the right tools, organizations can cultivate a healthier, more resilient work environment.

Chapter 26: The Importance of Personal Discipline

Introduction

Personal discipline is the foundation on which great achievements are built. It is the internal force that drives you to do what is necessary rather than what is comfortable or convenient. This chapter explores how personal discipline can transform your life, allowing you to achieve your goals and live in accordance with your deepest values.

Defining Personal Discipline

Discipline vs. Motivation: While motivation may fluctuate, discipline is constant. It is the long-term commitment to your goals, regardless of the emotions of the moment.

Self-discipline as a Habit: Personal discipline is a habit that is cultivated daily. It is the practice of exercising control over your actions, thoughts and emotions to intentionally direct your life.

Discipline as a Choice: Every day, we are faced with decisions that test our discipline. Choosing the option that brings us closer to our goals is an act of self-discipline.

Pillars of Personal Discipline

Clarity of Objectives: Having a clear vision of what you want to achieve is essential. Define your goals precisely and establish detailed action plans to achieve them.

Routines and Structure: Routines create the structure necessary for self-discipline. Establish daily routines that support your goals and keep you on track.

Time management: Personal discipline requires effective time management. Learn to prioritize tasks and say no to distractions that don't contribute to your goals.

Overcoming obstacles

Procrastination Management: Procrastination is the enemy of discipline. Develop strategies to overcome the tendency to procrastinate and stay focused on your most important tasks.

Resilience in the face of Failure: The road to success is full of failures. Personal discipline allows you to see failures as learning opportunities and move forward.

Balance between Discipline and Flexibility: While discipline is crucial, it is also important to be flexible. Adapt your methods and approaches when circumstances change.

Chapter 27: Developing Intuition for Decision Making

Introduction

Intuition is a powerful tool in decision making. Often described as a "sixth sense," intuition can offer invaluable guidance when logic alone is not enough. This chapter dives into how you can hone your intuition and use it to make more informed decisions aligned with your deepest values.

Understanding Intuition

Intuition vs. Instinct: While instinct is a biological response to a stimulus, intuition is deep knowledge that comes from experience and learning.

The Role of the Subconscious: Our subconscious processes information much faster than our conscious mind. Learning to listen to and trust these signals can improve our decision making.

Intuition and Emotion: Distinguishing between an emotional reaction and genuine intuition is key. Intuition is a calm, persistent sensation, not a sharp emotional response.

Cultivating Intuition

Mindfulness and Meditation: Practicing mindfulness and meditation can help calm the mind and clarify intuition.

Experience and Reflection: Intuition is strengthened with experience. Reflecting on past decisions and their results can be a valuable exercise in developing intuition.

Active listening: Learning to listen not only with your ears but with your entire being can open doors to intuition. Active listening involves being fully present and receptive to subtle cues.

Applying Intuition in Decision Making

Balance between Reason and Intuition: The best decision making occurs when intuition and reason work together. Learn to balance these two aspects to make more complete decisions.

Self Confidence: Trusting your intuition requires trust in yourself. Strengthen your self-confidence so you can trust your internal perceptions.

Intuition in Leadership: Effective leaders often use their intuition to guide their teams through uncertain or complex situations.

Chapter 28: Leadership in Times of Crisis

Introduction

Times of crisis are the true crucible for leaders. It is in these difficult times where authentic leadership is tested and revealed in its full capacity. This chapter addresses how leaders can navigate the turbulent waters of crisis, maintaining calm, clarity, and confidence in both themselves and their teams.

Understanding the Crisis

Nature of the Crisis: Recognizing that crisis can arise in many ways - economic, social, personal, or global - is the first step to managing it effectively.

Emotional Impact: Crises often bring with them a high degree of uncertainty and stress. Understanding the emotional impact on yourself and others is crucial.

Opportunities in the Crisis: While crises present challenges, they can also be opportunities for growth and innovation.

Principles of Leadership in Crisis

Clear and Transparent Communication: In times of crisis, effective communication is more important than ever. Leaders must be clear, honest and consistent in their communication.

Decisive Decision Making: The ability to make quick, well-informed decisions is essential. Leaders must balance agility with diligence.

Empathy and Support: Showing empathy and offering support to those affected by the crisis can strengthen morale and foster loyalty.

Strategies to Manage the Crisis

Risk Assessment and Contingency Planning: Preparing for the worst while hoping for the best is a prudent strategy. Leaders must assess risks and have contingency plans ready.

Collaborative Leadership: Crises require a team approach. Fostering collaboration and leveraging collective strengths can lead to innovative solutions.

Resilience and Adaptability: The ability to quickly recover and adapt to changing circumstances is a mark of great leadership.

Chapter 29: The Importance of Humility in Leadership

Introduction

Humility is an often underrated virtue in leadership. In a world that rewards confidence and assertiveness, humility can be seen as a weakness. However, it is precisely this quality that can make a leader genuinely great. This chapter explores humility not as a limitation, but as a powerful leadership tool.

Humility: The Heart of Servant Leadership

Defining Humility: Humility is the recognition of our own limitations and the openness to learn from others. It is a willingness to put the needs of others before one's own ambitions.

Servant Leadership: Servant leadership focuses on the well-being and growth of followers. A humble leader is dedicated to serving his team, not bossing him around.

Benefits of Humility: Humble leaders foster a collaborative and supportive work environment. Humility invites feedback, promotes learning and adaptability, and builds trusting relationships.

Humility and Decision Making

Recognition of the Contribution of Others: Humble leaders value and recognize the contributions of their team. This not only improves morale, but also leads to better collective decisions.

Admit Mistakes: Part of humility is admitting mistakes and learning from them. A leader who can do this demonstrates strength and earns the respect of his team.

Development of Others: Humility allows leaders to focus on developing and empowering their followers, leading to a stronger, more capable team.

Cultivating Humility in Leadership Practice

Self-reflection and Self-knowledge: Regular self-reflection is key to staying humble. Knowing your own strengths and weaknesses allows you to lead more authentically.

Active Listening: Humility manifests itself in the ability to listen actively. Humble leaders seek to truly understand the perspectives of others.

Mentoring and Continuous Learning: A humble leader is a lifelong learner. They seek mentors and learning opportunities to constantly improve.

Challenges and Rewards of Humility in Leadership

Balance between Humility and Confidence: Finding the right balance between being humble and projecting confidence is a challenge for many leaders.

Humility and Authority: Maintaining authority while being humble is another challenge. Leaders must learn to exercise their authority without arrogance.

Rewards of Humility: Despite the challenges, humility brings significant rewards. More united teams, wiser decisions and more effective leadership are just a few of them.

Chapter 30: Developing the Capacity to Influence Without Authority

Introduction

Influencing without authority is a crucial skill in today's interconnected world. Whether at work, in the community, or in personal relationships, the ability to influence others without relying on hierarchical power is a mark of true and effective leadership. This chapter focuses on how you can develop this skill to achieve positive results and build strong relationships.

Understanding Influence without Authority

Influence vs. Can: Influence is the ability to guide the decisions and behaviors of others, while power is based on formal authority. The influence is more subtle and often more effective.

The Psychology of Influence: Understanding the factors that motivate people and how they perceive authority is essential to effectively influence without exerting power.

The Role of Credibility: Credibility is the currency of influence. Building and maintaining credibility is essential to being influential without authority.

Strategies to Influence without Authority

Build Relationships: Strong relationships are the foundation of influence. Investing time in knowing and understanding people increases your ability to influence them.

Effective communication: The ability to communicate ideas clearly and convincingly is key. Influence often begins with the ability to present your ideas in a way that resonates with others.

Active Listening and Empathy: Showing genuine interest and understanding in others' perspectives allows you to influence them more effectively.

Applying Influence in Various Contexts

In the workplace: Learn to influence colleagues and superiors to promote collaboration and innovation.

In the Community: Uses influence to mobilize resources and support for community causes.

On Social Networks: Expand your reach and influence through digital platforms, where formal authority is less relevant.

Challenges and Ethics of Influence

Navigating Organizational Politics: Influence without authority can be complicated in highly hierarchical environments. Learning to navigate organizational politics is crucial.

Maintaining Integrity: It is important to influence without manipulating. Integrity and ethics should be central to your efforts to influence others.

Balancing Influence and Collaboration: While you seek to influence, you must also be open to being influenced. The balance between giving and receiving is essential for mutually beneficial relationships.

Chapter 31: The Importance of Clarity and Simplicity

Introduction

In an increasingly complex and information-saturated world, clarity and simplicity have become essential elements for effective leadership. These qualities not only improve communication and decision making, but also make it easier to understand and execute strategies. This chapter explores how leaders can apply clarity and simplicity to improve their influence and effectiveness.

Clarity in Thought and Communication

Definition of Clarity: Clarity implies being easily understood. Clear thinking leads to clear communication, which is essential for leadership.

Techniques to Improve Clarity: Using simple language, structuring information logically, and avoiding jargon are key techniques to improve clarity.

Benefits of Clarity: Clarity allows teams to quickly understand goals and expectations, leading to better alignment and execution.

Simplicity in Strategy and Execution

Definition of Simplicity: Simplicity is the practice of making something as efficient and free of excess as possible.

Strategies to Simplify: Identifying and eliminating unnecessary processes, focusing on what is essential, and delegating effectively are strategies to simplify.

Impact of Simplicity: Simplicity in strategy and execution can lead to greater agility and adaptability.

Applying Clarity and Simplicity in Leadership

Behavior Modeling: Leaders must model clarity and simplicity in their own behavior to inspire others to do the same.

Team Development: Fostering an environment where clarity and simplicity are valued can improve collaboration and innovation.

Change management: Applying clarity and simplicity in change management can facilitate the transition and acceptance by teams.

Challenges and Considerations

Balance between Simplicity and Depth: Finding the balance between keeping things simple and not oversimplifying is a challenge for leaders.

Clarity in Times of Uncertainty: Maintaining clarity when there is uncertainty requires constant and transparent communication.

Organizational culture: Organizational culture can resist simplicity if it is used to complexity. Leaders must work to change this mindset.

Chapter 32: Developing Strategic Patience

Introduction

Strategic patience is an essential virtue in leadership and personal life. It's not about simply waiting, but doing so with purpose and an understanding that time can be a powerful ally. This chapter explores how to cultivate strategic patience and apply it to achieve long-term goals and overcome challenges.

Understanding Strategic Patience

Definition of Strategic Patience: Strategic patience is the ability to tolerate delays or setbacks while staying focused on long-term goals.

Patience as a Resource: Patience is a resource that, when used strategically, can lead to more informed decisions and more successful results.

Benefits of Strategic Patience: Strategic patience allows for better evaluation of situations, reduces impulsive decision making, and can build respect and trust in others.

Developing Strategic Patience

Self-awareness and Emotional Control: The development of self-awareness and emotional control are essential for strategic patience. Recognizing and managing your emotions allows you to remain calm and clear.

Goal Setting and Planning: Setting clear goals and a detailed action plan can help you maintain patience by providing a roadmap for success.

Stress Management Techniques: Learning and practicing stress management techniques such as meditation, exercise, and conscious breathing can improve your ability to be patient.

Applying Strategic Patience

In Leadership: Leaders with strategic patience can guide their teams through periods of uncertainty and change while maintaining the long-term vision.

In making decisions: Strategic patience allows you to make more informed decisions, waiting for the right information and the right moment.

In Personal Life: Applying strategic patience in your personal life can lead to deeper relationships and personal satisfaction.

Challenges and Overcoming

Culture of Immediacy: We live in a culture that values speed and immediacy. Learning to resist this pressure and remain patient is a challenge.

Balance between Patience and Action: Finding the balance between being patient and taking action is crucial. Strategic patience is not inaction, but informed and timely action.

Patience and perseverance: Strategic patience is closely linked to perseverance. Developing both qualities is essential to overcome obstacles and achieve success.

Chapter 33: Leadership and the Importance of Passion

Introduction

Passion is the fuel that drives leaders to achieve excellence and inspire others to follow their vision. It is not just about enthusiasm or energy, but about a deep commitment to a purpose that transcends personal interests. This chapter examines how passion in leadership can be a powerful catalyst for change and innovation.

Passion as a Cornerstone of Leadership

Definition of Passion: Passion is an intense emotion that motivates and gives direction to our actions. In leadership, it is what drives perseverance and dedication.

Identifying your Passion: Understanding what you are passionate about is the first step to integrating that passion into your leadership. Self-exploration and reflection can help you identify your true passions.

Passion and Vision: Passion is contagious and can instill a shared vision that mobilizes people toward a common goal.

Cultivating Passion in Yourself and Others

Personal development: Passion is nurtured through personal and professional growth. Leaders must continually seek opportunities to expand their skills and knowledge.

Inspiring Passion in the Team: Leaders can inspire passion in their teams by aligning organizational goals with individual interests and motivations.

Recognition and Celebration: Celebrating achievements and recognizing effort fosters passion and commitment within a team.

Passion and its Impact on Organizational Culture

Culture of Passion: An organizational culture that values passion fosters innovation and creativity. Leaders must work to create an environment that supports and encourages passion.

Passion and Work Ethic: Passion can lead to a strong work ethic and a commitment to excellence. Leaders must model this behavior to set a high standard.

Passion Management: While passion is beneficial, it must also be managed to avoid burnout. Leaders must balance passion with well-being and sustainability.

Challenges and Rewards of Passion in Leadership

Balance between Passion and Pragmatism: Leaders must find a balance between following their passion and being pragmatic in their decisions and strategies.

Passion and Resilience: Passion can be a source of resilience in difficult times. Leaders must cultivate passion as a resource to overcome challenges.

Passion and Legacy: Passion in leadership not only affects the present, but can also leave a lasting legacy. Leaders must consider how their passion will influence the future of their organization.

Chapter 34: The Importance of Consistency in Leadership

Introduction

Consistency is a fundamental pillar of effective leadership. It not only provides a sense of stability and predictability in organizations but also strengthens a leader's trust and credibility. This chapter breaks down how consistency impacts all areas of leadership and how leaders can cultivate it to improve their influence and effectiveness.

Consistency as the Foundation of Leadership

Definition of Consistency: Consistency in leadership refers to the alignment between words and actions, as well as regularity in behavior and decisions.

Consistency and Trust: Consistency is essential to building and maintaining trust. Followers trust leaders who are predictable in their principles and actions.

Consistency and Organizational Culture: Consistent leadership establishes the norms and expectations that form the culture of an organization.

Developing Consistency in Leadership

Self-discipline and Routines: Self-discipline and establishing routines are key to developing consistency. Leaders must practice what they preach and be role models.

Clear and Transparent Communication: Maintaining clear and transparent communication helps leaders be consistent in their message and direction.

Expectation Management: Setting and managing clear expectations with the team ensures that everyone is aligned and understands common goals.

Applying Consistency in Leadership Practice

In making decisions: Consistency in decision making reinforces trust in leadership and allows teams to adapt and respond effectively.

In Conflict Management: Being consistent in handling conflict demonstrates fairness and fairness, which is crucial to maintaining morale and respect.

In Team Development: Consistency in team development and training ensures continuous growth and improvement.

Challenges and Strategies to Maintain Consistency

Changes and Adaptability: Leaders must balance the need for consistency with the ability to adapt to change. Flexibility must not compromise fundamental consistency.

Consistency vs. Rigidity: Avoiding rigidity is important; Consistency does not mean inflexibility. Leaders must be consistent in their values, but flexible in their approach.

Evaluation and Feedback: Regular self-assessment and seeking feedback can help leaders stay on the path to consistency.

Chapter 35: Developing the Skill of Active Listening

Introduction

The skill of active listening is one of the most powerful tools in a leader's arsenal. It's not just about hearing the words being said, but about fully understanding the message being conveyed. This chapter focuses on how leaders can develop and hone the skill of active listening to improve communication, relationships, and decision making.

Active Listening at the Core of Effective Leadership

Definition of Active Listening: Active listening involves paying full attention to the speaker, understanding their message, responding appropriately, and retaining information.

Benefits of Active Listening: Improves understanding, fosters trust and respect, and promotes an environment of openness and honesty.

Active Listening vs. Passive Listening: Unlike passive listening, active listening is a dynamic process that requires conscious effort and participation.

Developing Active Listening

Barrier Awareness: Identifying and overcoming personal barriers such as prejudices, distractions and premature judgments is essential for active listening.

Key Skills: Developing skills such as patience, empathy and concentration are essential to becoming an active listener.

Practice and Feedback: Consistent practice and seeking feedback can significantly improve active listening skills.

Applying Active Listening in Various Contexts

In Team Leadership: Using active listening to understand the team's needs and concerns can lead to better management and leadership.

In Conflict Resolution: Active listening is crucial in conflict resolution, as it allows all parties to feel heard and understood.

In making decisions: Making informed decisions requires actively listening to all perspectives and carefully considering them.

Challenges and Strategies to Improve Active Listening

Multitasking and Distractions: In a world full of distractions, learning to focus solely on the speaker is a challenge that leaders must overcome.

Development of Patience: Patience is vital for active listening. Leaders should work on developing the patience to listen without interrupting or rushing the speaker.

Constructive Feedback: Giving and receiving constructive feedback can help identify areas of improvement in active listening.

Chapter 36: The Importance of Flexibility and Openness to Change

Introduction

In a world that is changing at an unprecedented pace, flexibility and openness to change are not only desirable qualities, but essential for effective leadership. These characteristics allow leaders to adapt and thrive in dynamic and often uncertain environments. This chapter explores how flexibility and openness to change can be cultivated and applied to lead successfully in the modern era.

Flexibility: The Ability to Adapt

Definition of Flexibility: Flexibility is the ability to change or be changed easily to adapt to new circumstances.

Flexibility and Creativity: Flexibility fosters creativity, allowing leaders to think of innovative and out-of-the-box solutions.

Flexibility as a Competitive Advantage: In today's market, flexibility can be a significant competitive advantage, allowing organizations to move quickly and capitalize on new opportunities.

Openness to Change: Accept the New

Definition of Openness to Change: Openness to change implies a positive disposition towards transformation and evolution, both personal and organizational.

Openness to Change and Learning: Openness to change is intrinsically linked to continuous learning. Leaders who embrace change are often lifelong learners.

Change management: Openness to change is crucial to effective change management, ensuring transitions are managed in ways that support growth and development.

Developing Flexibility and Openness to Change

Cultivate a Growth Mindset: A growth mindset is the foundation for developing both flexibility and openness to change.

Adaptability Strategies: Developing strategies to adapt to different situations helps leaders stay flexible and open to change.

Practice and Experience: Exposure to diverse situations and conscious practice of adaptability improve flexibility and openness to change.

Challenges and Strategies to Maintain Flexibility and Openness to Change

Overcome Resistance to Change: Resistance to change is a common challenge. Leaders must find ways to overcome this resistance and foster a culture of adaptability.

Balance between Stability and Change: Finding the right balance between stability and change is essential to avoid unnecessary disruption.

Communication and Collaboration: Effective communication and collaboration are essential to facilitate flexibility and openness to change throughout the organization.

Chapter 37: Developing the Skill to Recognize and Celebrate Accomplishments

Introduction

Recognition and celebration of achievements are crucial aspects of leadership that contribute significantly to team motivation and morale. This chapter focuses on how leaders can develop the ability to identify and celebrate both big successes and small triumphs, creating a culture of appreciation and recognition.

The Importance of Recognition

Definition of Recognition: Recognition involves validation and appreciation of the efforts and achievements of individuals and teams.

Impact of Recognition on Motivation: Appropriate recognition can increase motivation and engagement, and encourage repetition of positive behaviors.

Talent Recognition and Retention: A culture of recognition can improve talent retention by making employees feel valued and part of something bigger than themselves.

Developing the Skill of Recognition

Active Observation and Attention to Details: Leaders must develop the ability to actively observe and pay attention to details to identify achievements worthy of recognition.

Effective Communication of Recognition: Learning to communicate recognition effectively, whether publicly or privately, is essential for recognition to be meaningful.

Personalization of Recognition: Personalizing recognition to align with what is important to the individual can make recognition more impactful.

Celebrating Achievements

Celebration Planning: Plan and execute celebrations that reflect the importance of achievements and are inclusive for the entire team.

Consistent and Timely Celebrations: Consistency and timeliness in celebrating achievements ensure that recognition is relevant and timely.

Feedback Incorporation: Including constructive feedback along with recognition can provide an opportunity for continued growth and development.

Challenges and Strategies for Recognition and Celebration

Avoid Favoritism: Leaders must be mindful of avoiding favoritism and ensuring that recognition is fair and equitable.

Recognition in Difficult Times: Finding reasons to celebrate and recognize achievements even in difficult times can be challenging, but it's crucial to keeping morale high.

Measuring the Impact of Recognition: Developing methods to measure the impact of recognition on morale and productivity can help fine-tune recognition and celebration strategies.

www.ingramcontent.com/pod-product-compliance
Lightning Source LLC
Chambersburg PA
CBHW050013230526
45470CB00003B/949